BROKEN TOGETHER

BROKEN TOGETHER

A Minister's Daughter

ALEXANDRA COE

RESOURCE *Publications* · Eugene, Oregon

BROKEN TOGETHER
A Minister's Daughter

Copyright © 2022 Alexandra Coe. All rights reserved. Except for brief quotations in critical publications or reviews, no part of this book may be reproduced in any manner without prior written permission from the publisher. Write: Permissions, Wipf and Stock Publishers, 199 W. 8th Ave., Suite 3, Eugene, OR 97401.

Resource Publications
An Imprint of Wipf and Stock Publishers
199 W. 8th Ave., Suite 3
Eugene, OR 97401

www.wipfandstock.com

PAPERBACK ISBN: 978-1-6667-3253-5
HARDCOVER ISBN: 978-1-6667-2635-0
EBOOK ISBN: 978-1-6667-2636-7

.   JANUARY 4, 2022 8:52 AM

For Luke and Eowyn

CONTENTS

Preface | ix

Introduction | xi

———

Genealogy | 1

The Fall: A Drama | 2

Tamzen Donner Speaks | 6

The Flaming Sword: A Treacherous Beckoning,
The Sign of the Curse, and a Cross | 8

The Grass is Always Greener | 10

Empathy for the Spider | 11

Westward Ho: The Animals Speak | 12

Ma-To-Toh-Pa ("Four Bears", Fur Trader,
Mandan Tribe, 1784–1837, Dakota Territory) | 13

COVID 19, April 2020 | 14

To the Churches in Exile | 15

Communion | 16

College Romance | 17

Short Stay in the Psych Ward #1 | 18

Short Stay in the Psych Ward #2—The Day Room | 20

Praeparatio: An Advent Sermon | 24

Drybones (Ezekiel 37:1–14) | 26

The Tipsy Parson | 30

The Inter-Testamental Period | 31

Melanie | 32

How Many Likes? | 33

This Little Thing | 34

Natural Born World Shaker, "Cool Hand Luke" | 35

Tombs of Two Generals | 37

War Machine | 38

Casualty | 40

American Guns | 41

The Impeccable Logic of James Holmes
(The "Dark Knight" Killer) | 42

Lost Time | 43

A Conversation: The Woman at the Well | 44

12 Step Meeting | 48

Survivor—An Imaginary Therapist's Notes | 49

Chance Meeting of Poets on the Street | 51

Sober | 52

Three Undiscovered Tudor Manuscripts | 53

We, The Women | 56

Child of God? | 59

One Step Ahead—Like a Rolling Stone | 60

PREFACE

People often say that there are two kinds of Preachers' Kids, the "good" and the "bad", the docile and the rebellious, the straight arrows and the twisted souls. The truth is that we are all a little bit of both, as our parents were. In this we are no different from anyone, from the Golden Child to the scapegoat.

"For every valley will be lifted up, and every mountain and hill brought to even ground; the crooked will straighten, and roughness smoothed."
(Isaiah 40:45)

INTRODUCTION

THIS A MULTI-GENRE WORK including poems, prose poems, and essays, punctuated by biblical reflections in poetic or dramatic form. Where biblical passages are quoted, I have provided my own translation. The work's primary aim is to explore the topics of mental health and addiction as they affect clergy, their families, and, I hope, any reader, whether a person of faith or no faith. I also include reflections on cultural and global issues such as war, gun violence, and sexual molestation. My hope is to effectively blur the distinction between sacred and secular and to be a voice for the voiceless, so that all readers may be able to find themselves reflected here, in their pain and in their hope.

GENEALOGY

I stand on the shoulders of giants
who spoke about the Light but were silent about the Dark
even as they surveyed the landscape of the lost.
I am the giant who will tell the stories of the dark
to complete the work of my forefathers and foremothers
even if some of them reach out from death and try to cover my mouth
I will speak, and the people who need to hear
will hear.
I will find them
and bring them home.

THE FALL: A DRAMA

Then the Lord God said to the human,

You may eat of any tree in the garden but the tree of knowledge of good and evil, for when you do you shall necessarily die.

The Lord God said, it is not good for the human to be alone. I will make the human a helper (. . .) And Adam and Eve were both naked, and they felt no shame.

Now the serpent was more cunning than any of the animals God had made. He said to Eve, Did God really say, you must not eat from any tree in the garden? And Eve said to the serpent, We may eat fruit from the trees in the garden, but God did say, You must not eat from the tree that is in the middle of the garden, and you must not touch it, or you will die.

You will not necessarily die, the serpent said to the woman. For God knows that when you eat of it, your eyes will be opened and you will be like God, knowing good and evil.

When Eve saw that the tree was good for food and pleasing to the eye, she took some and ate it, and gave it to Adam, and he ate.

Then the eyes of both were opened, and they realized they were naked. So they sewed fig leaves together, and made themselves clothing. (. . .)

To the woman Good said,

I will greatly increase your pain in childbearing; in pain you shall bring forth children. Your desire shall be for your husband, and he shall rule over you.

To Adam God said (. . .)

Cursed is the ground because of you. Through painful toil you shall eat of it all the days of your life (. . .) By the sweat of your brow, you will eat your food, all the days of your life, until you return to the ground from which you were taken (. . .)

After God drove humanity out, God placed on the east side of the garden of Eden cherubim and a flaming sword flashing back and forth to guard the way to the tree of Life.

(Genesis 3)

(Enter: Adam and Eve)

(Adam and Eve:)
We are together, here, in this place.
It is clear above; sometimes, pure water comes down.

(Eve:)
There are living beings growing from the earth.
Some of them are tall with hard skins, and reach up to the sky.
They shelter us from the water that comes down.
Some are small and tender. Their fragrance makes us glad.
We allow
these beings to grow.

(Adam:)
There are other beings here, not like us.
They look and walk differently. They are our friends.

(Eve:)
I look at you, and you make my heart glad.

(Adam:)
Your skin is warm to my touch.

(Adam and Eve:)
With you, I am not alone. We help each other.
That Great One who walks among us gave us all of this.
We do as That One says. To do this makes us glad.
We may eat of all the trees but that one.
The One who walks among us knows why these things are so.
There is no more we need to have, or know.

(Enter: Serpent)

(Serpent:)
Can you be so sure? Are you so sure you understood the words?
You are so naïve. Why do you take everything at face value?
This place isn't good enough for you. Do what you want.
Can't you think independently? Certainly you are capable of asking
a question. What did that one say?

(Eve:)
The words were "Do not eat, don't even touch!"
And something about the "middle of the garden (. . .)"
I'm not so sure anymore.

(Adam:)
Did that One say, Don't even touch? I don't think so (. . .)

(Adam and Eve:)
I don't remember now.

(They turn away from each other. The light dims.)

(Adam:)
I just had a beautiful dream.
I can't quite remember what it was.

(Eve:)
Something has changed. Has everything changed?
I hear your voice but you sound like a stranger.

(Adam:)
I can't look at you now, and I don't know why.

(Adam and Eve:)
Why do I feel so alone? And so ashamed?

(Eve:)
I feel something new towards you that I have never felt. Something pure
has gone, all that is left is fear mixed with
desire, and I know you will give me pain.

(Adam:)
You are still beautiful, but now perhaps not beautiful enough.
I want to keep you, to possess you, and have you do
as I wish, as all these other beings should.

(Eve:)
Your face is suddenly all full of care; you've been working
too hard.

(Adam and Eve:)
Once we loved it here; now everything is ruined. There is no
point in staying here any more.
Can we ever get back to the way it was before?
How do we shut off this noise in our heads, the words that
whisper,
This is not enough?

Will we ever dream that dream again?
There is no choice now. We must go.

(Exeunt, separately. in opposite directions)

TAMZEN DONNER SPEAKS*

Hastings swore, saying
he knew that road like the back of his hand.
I warned our little band, early in the journey,
But being only a woman I was ignored. Not surprising.
Even from the grave, I tell you,
I know not what was done with my body. I always said,
even before we started,
I'd do anything to save my children.
I ate only for strength and to protect them. We pioneer women
were not particularly pious, but we remembered the words from church,

This is my body. This is my blood.

We had at least one scruple, because all others had been stripped away:
We would never eat our own . . . though in the end
Flesh tastes like flesh, and meat like meat, and we were insane
from cold and fear, snowbound and snowblind,
almost past caring.

Who are you then, the soft ones, to judge, to be so sure
what you would never have done in my position?
You too have ignored clear warnings, and trusted the wrong men.
Easy for you to call us fools, while you too follow arrogant blind men
down the shortcut way to death and horror.
You too, use and consume everything in your path
To reach the beckoning will-o'-the-wisp of a false paradise.
You are so sure the road will lead you there. You, too
should have stayed.

---

* Tamzen Donner was a member of the Donner Party. She was the only one of the party who warned against taking Hastings Cutoff, the route which was advocated by Lansford Hastings, and which, in large part, led them to disaster in the winter of 1846–1847.

The disaster that plagues you now
has separated the heroes from those others.

You too, must navigate your own perilous journey, as we did.

And now the question is for you:
Would you do anything
To save your children?

THE FLAMING SWORD:
A TREACHEROUS BECKONING,
THE SIGN OF THE CURSE, AND A CROSS

The flaming sword placed by the angels on the edge of Eden is the sign of humanity's permanent state of exile, a vicious circle repeated continually throughout history. Doomed by the very nature of our own transgression—a despising of our own simple contentment and gratitude, banished and now forever lost, trying to get home but always the wrong way, as in a child's recurring nightmare — we are forced to heed yet another will-o'-the-wisp, a terrible cutting light, Macbeth's dagger of the mind, flashing all ways like a neon sign at the door of the gambling house where we once again lose all. We can't lay a finger of a memory on where or when this all went wrong, but we made a mistake, and despised that happiness. That we know.

This is the point at which some Christian interpreters will feel tempted to say quickly, Ah, but the flaming sword is Christ, don't you see? We must resist that temptation for a moment, and not leap to eisegesis and the magical production of Jesus' name, a name which these writers did not know. That would be yet another flaming sword, a quicker way, a cutting away of the difficulty with which this text presents us on its own terms. We must pause and let the painful sword cut for a moment (. . .) cut like the knife lodged in the heart of a suffering poet ("Here's one from 1964. Can't you take this 1964 one from me?" (Charles Bukowski, "Man mowing his lawn across the street from me"), echoing yet another, earlier suffering poet who begged the insanely repetitive memory of grief to leave the door of his heart ("The Raven", Edgar A. Poe).

We may turn for comfort from this darkness and pain to the words from the gospel of John: "For the light shines in the darkness, and the darkness has not overcome it." (John 1:3). This text upon reflection may not be as comforting as we wish. The text does not say, "For the light has shined in the darkness, and the darkness has been completely obliterated, and the whole world has been flooded with dazzling brightness." No — when we read "The darkness has not overcome it," there is a whisper of an unspoken word: Yet. Life with and in Christ is a rugged road that we must tread, often with no light visible, feeling our way along with the knowledge that any flickering lights we may think we see are as false as those of Plato's cave. Through the only law that we can still choose if we are broken enough, the law of Love, we can only make improvements, make amends, not fix our broken state but enter a strange new land of suffering together (. . .) so that Eve may wipe her husband's sweat at the end of a long day and cry with him, so that Adam may hold the hand of his wife in the agony of childhood and in the toil of her own birthing, and rejoice with her, so that together they may shush the cries of the New Man born once again in darkness and in exile, teaching them a new thing: Sacrifice.

"For while we hope for what we do not see, we wait for it with patience" (Romans 8:2).

THE GRASS IS ALWAYS GREENER

Not someone else's field or barn
will yield my crop, not another's life
glimpsed from outside can soothe the aching wish
    a mirage mocking my reach.

No, my life, my own, its awkward shape
contains in this imperfect moment
This landscape, replete with my hopes and joys—-
the dog crouched in the grass
the children who walk and sing with me
the man with whom I live in struggle and in love
the self with whom I dance in rejection and embrace

My crop is rich and filling
For it is mine.

EMPATHY FOR THE SPIDER

In the late 1950s, a spider made its home in the upper left-hand corner of the front door of our house in New Hampshire. This part of the house was built in the early 1800s and faced north toward the Presidential Range of the White Mountains. On one of those crystal summer days you could just barely make out Mount Washington.

The house is sold, now. My grandparents are buried just a hundred yards or so down the road in a cemetery ground rolling with age. One of the graves is from the Revolutionary War. The spider lodged in the corner of the door. It presided over the front room with a grand piano, where we would sit by the fire during the cool nights and pop popcorn over the fire and play charades. We would leave despondently at the end of every summer (. . .) leave the glorious blue and gold behind, heading back to our colorless suburb in the Midwest. The spider stayed, guarding the house, alone through the bleak New Hampshire winters, year after year, hearing no sound but the wind moaning and thrilling there, feeling the aching bones of the house left there, the spider and the house both left in mute cold consolation. I don't know what happened to the spider, but I know it was gone by the day that my new and now gone husband danced in that room after the wedding. I don't remember what the music was.

WESTWARD HO: THE ANIMALS SPEAK

This used to be our land. I roamed here with my brothers and sisters
hunting for food in this vast space
waiting in the still moonlight of the prairie and the deep canyon silences
hidden by high brush and cactus

but I feel a shift in the air
I smell something coming, it has foul breath and leaves a smoke
black like the night but tinged with a strange green sickness
What is this strange animal moving at a pace I have not seen
cutting a swath through this land, our home?
It makes me wary. I must run and hide
learn its tricks and its habits,
run from the creatures with loud exploding sticks.
They are not our friends.

I sense an awful thing. The beginning of the end
of our life lived together. Maybe if we run past that next ridge, we will be
    safe.
But I know the new Rulers will leave a wasteland.
They will dig until there is nothing left to dig
take until there is nothing left to take.
and I know
Soon we must go.

MA-TO-TOH-PA
("FOUR BEARS", FUR TRADER, MANDAN TRIBE, 1784–1837, DAKOTA TERRITORY)

I took you for my wife in this land that was ours
your skin brown in the sun
your black hair lustrous and adorned
with red, gold, and azure beads.
All the people approved, and we were happy.
We made friends with the white men
who came, fur trappers and men from the east with pockets of coins
But the white men killed all the beaver for their pelts and brought us sickness
and now I am dying of a pox
so rotten the wolves will not eat me

So we will lie down in the dust
And say goodbye to this vast island. We never said we owned it.
All that we leave behind they will take
And there will come one who will dance and prophesy
a bad spirit
descending on these men, women and children, soon and very soon
Plagues brought on by strangers
will destroy them too.

COVID 19, APRIL 2020

It's a mid-April Saturday afternoon
cloudy and warm, quieter than usual on this post-industrial street.
(Feels more like a Sunday, but then, the days
keep getting mixed up. I know you feel it too.)

We're all trying to find a breath behind our masks
trying to hold our heads above this sickening fume
that haunts America in 2020.

Where will be the joy in Easter?
Or are we stuck in a liturgical loop of Good Friday?—
caught in perpetual mourning, weeping at the foot of the Cross
for the careless and entirely preventable
slaughter of the innocents
in a diaspora of the people so broad
that we can no longer see each other, and I may not touch your hand?

TO THE CHURCHES IN EXILE

How empty is thy dwelling place
O Lord thou God of the hundred millions,
remnants of your plagued people now in exile
bereft of communion, potluck suppers, the handshake of the pastor.

Those who are dying will die,
says the online prophet.
Says the Lord: Those who join Me in sacrifice
will live on the daily manna of taped sermons and Zoom prayer groups
a sip of wine, a bite of bread in real time
at the video's time stamp
from the abandonment of a lonely living room.

There can no longer be
a question of my real Presence everywhere.
Where two or three are gathered I am there
with every "like" and "share".

COMMUNION

Holding you was the taking and the giving
of the sacrament of pain
body to body, blood to blood
heart to heart in grief's arterial pulse.

My breath, questioning, listened
with the half-hope of the moribund
for some word of transubstantiation
some hierophantic whisper
that this common pain's obscenity
might at long last be sanctified by meaning

As when the priest lifts up the host, and prays,
and benediction may at last be spoken
and the muttering congregation of lost ones
may return home.

COLLEGE ROMANCE

The college kid kisses her goodbye at the bus stop. He is careful to allot the right number of kisses to her, enough so that when she turns to leave she tastes his taste on her mouth, and wipes her longnailed fingers in exasperation across her thigh, like that's where she wants his fingers to be resting, tracing. She would give anything to keep him, for just one more night.

SHORT STAY IN THE PSYCH WARD #1

Truth's in your corner.
It's roughly defined by the parameter of your desk.
Behind it, the big erasable bulletin board, patients' names, last names first,
and the appropriate categories, level 2 or 3 which dictate
    whether we can go outside. There is no level 1.

Truth's in your corner
being a med student, if female, shielded from your own terror
by a massive jellohunk of extra fat so common among female health care workers
    godknowswhy.
If male, cleanshaven in your cocksure twenties and
more or less fresh from a too-clinging drama queen of a girlfriend
    who's a little crazy herself,
at an age when pain is something still so surface you've only skimmed it
    like a bird skims waves far inland bobbing on the waters.
Suffering comes much later.

You take notes, not discreetly enough, as we have our lunch.
We cry reduced to the petulant tears of an exhausted five-year-old
when there's no mayonnaise for our overly salted tuna fish salad
served punctually at 5 o'clock. (who the hell eats dinner at 5 o'clock?)
You scribble notes now, more furtively. (Why do you think we're crying?)
You condescend out of your own brute panic when
I beg humiliated at age 45 for a second birdhouse to paint for my other kid
only to be told: one birdhouse per patient
and I break down crying in front of these other so-called crazies
whom I would prefer not to be in the same room with,
much less with you, the OT group
"facilitator", nice person as your undoubtedly are on the outside where we
    are equal,
where your own neuroses have been
rendered invisible to everyone, and most especially to you yourself.

That is the function of the Categories, bipolar, schizoaffective, borderline.
They promote, establish and promulgate and perpetuate
a false system of the
omnipotent Subject (you, the Health Care Expert),
as over against the passive and weak Object (we, the patients),
who open our mouths at medication time
and stick out our idiot tongues to receive the Host of Hosts
of Zyprexa, Neurontin, Wellbutrin, Depakote, Zoloft and Paxil
and are never taught, and never think to take responsibility for our own bodies,
for ourselves, to rise up, to care, to act, to think beyond,
to envision a world in which we might transcend the Categories
of textbook pain to which we have been so reduced
    and to which we have reduced ourselves

Like an image of what looks almost like a human being, barely discernible across the room
from the vague and blurred perspective of a nodding out med student
who's been awake for a mind-bending 72 hours
jotting barely coherent notes
behind a desk.

SHORT STAY IN THE PSYCH WARD #2—
THE DAY ROOM

Here lie the professionally insane
glued to the casual brutality of "Copshow"
thumbing through cut-up two-year-old copies of "Better Homes and
  Gardens"
banal outposts of that self-same thing that fashioned their stupefied
madness
the culture of their own exile, the gods
to which even now they cling in clueless obeisance
(personally, I'd prefer a Bach partita).

For them, this nothingness of locked-away razors and emasculate coffee
is a vacation
an occasional routine hiatus
from godknowswhat sickening alienation
to which after their due 72 hours they inevitably return.

The People

Romie

First thing I saw when I walked into the ward a second time around
was this entrancing sight:
6'2" septuagenarian black dude in a 3 piece cheap blue suit
matching his blue psycho-hospital slippers. Very impressive.
Romie spoke rapid fire Nawth Kah-lahnah or some such dialect.
He saw me raiding "his" peanut butter stash
That actually belongs to all the patients in the unit.
He sidles over and grumbles, "Stealin' mah peanut butter? You rat!"
Guy must consume three jars of Skippy Creamy Lite daily.
That's why you can hardly understand a word he say,
The fact that it's all slimed on to his palate and he don't wear his partials
  —tryin' to impress the ladies.

Romie usually tries to take you hostage in conversation, especially if you a lady,
That is, unless you give him the slightest reason to hate you.
You see, his father left everything he had to Romie's two sisters
    and left Romie nothing,
That's why he hoards everything, even the little packets of salt and pepper that are there for everyone in the unit.
That's why he hoards all the peanut butter too.
Calls hisself a blagass and a blagass mothaf****in n***ah..
Being curious. I ask, "What if a white person called you that?"
He says, "Welcome to it, love it, anytime," and then proceeds to tell the heartwarming story
of some white woman at a dinner party who
starts up calling him a blagass mothahf*****in n****ah
And he takes his open hand and smacks her across the face 'til it turns rayd, beet rayd
and about a separate occasion with an altogether different woman
of whose body he's enthusiastically availin' hisself
and she say, Oh, Oh! You bigass n***ah!
and he jumps up, takes a baseball bat conveniently by the bed
and jes' cracks her upside the hayd, pulls the sheet over her and takes off.
"Did she die?" "I dunno," was the apathetic shrug

And I say, "yeah, I probably won't be calling you a . . . you know.
Excuse me, I have to go to the bathroom," not having to go at all.
"I'll wait all night," says the three-piece-suited man, coquettishly.

Janice

Chunky, tan, long dark hair
Eyes on the TV screen, with occasional sidelong looks at me
    her "competition" in a room of madmen
Spitting snidely in response to CNN ads about baby products
"I'm not a mother, or a grandmother!" (but she is)
and returns to coloring valentines.

Scott

Football-obsessed
Jets hat and sweatshirt
Says "OH SHIT" at the opposing team's fumble
grasping for salvation at a yellow paper
    as his bet goes down the drain.

Jimmy

Legs planted, hat squarely placed
he stands like a security guard
anxious to encapsulate everyone's invisible truth
with an insipid rhyme
("I guess my biggest crime
Is straining to rhyme.")

Debra

Lies on her perpetually unmade bed
strewn with the melancholia of paper-bag belongings
She falls into mumbling medicated sleep
then harkens to "God's" wake-up call at 2:30 AM
And next morning hollowly recounts a litany
of shock treatments and bottles of Ativan
("That coma was really nice, so peaceful.
Makes you want it, mmmm.")

Then just lies there, twitching..

Jeffery

"When I was born I could hardly walk."

John

Having by 2 minutes
escaped pill-induced annihilation
He emits a stream of disconnected self-analysis,
beaming a smile.

———

In this purgatory, I find myself asking, what am I?—
—now that my own sharp edges that had jutted up like magnificent
mountains
    defined by the valley's very depths
have now been dulled by the smooth contours
of state-of-the-art
    mood stabilizers
    antidepressants
    antipsychotics
They will take me away!, I say in slurred protest
as I try to stamp my foot in a pathetic simulation
    of my once-glorious rebellion.

Somehow, we are together
The community of the broken
joined by our very estrangement
via the rejection of the
seemingly intact.

PRAEPARATIO: AN ADVENT SERMON

(Mark 1:3–4/ Matthew 3:1–3/ Luke 3:4–6)

Make way! was the cry or so was the story of old
sounding shrill across the sandblasted desert
the desert blasting sand sharp across the ear:
Prepare the way of the Lord! Clear a straight path for Him.

Pause for the moment, and ask: what is the nature of this proclamation?
We've heard it every year of our lives, from our baptism,
those words spoken every year
in every wreathed candlelit Advent service
    its meaning dulled by years of repetition —
forgetting that it is anything but facile.

What a prodigious task, this levelling of our paths!
What does the Baptist mean, that we must accomplish this ourselves?
We've already tried (. . .) and what an awful task it is.
The lifting up of this tiny sagging of the heart
that precisely fails to be lifted up, just where we so mightily pull and tug
and heroically will it to be lifted up
The load which every morning we resignedly shoulder
like a yoked animal who cannot begin to imagine
another sort of existence than its own.

We can lift it awhile longer, we say to ourselves.
"Prepare the way of the Lord"? What can we do?
And what about our pride, that screams we are self-sufficient
Our inability to forgive no matter how we much we think we have done so
Our clinging to the wounds and illusions that we think define us?
How can we level these mountains?

Make his paths straight. The task was all but impossible.

The sound of the task
was the lifting and the creaking and the straining
of a World being lifted up
on crude hinges, on a hill,
the sound of the breaking of the greatest Heart.

And then we see, perhaps the preparation is
to stop trying
to step once again into the river.
Let the water wash over you
Confess that you are uneven
That you are rough in places
That you cannot, try as you may, lift yourself up
That you cannot, try as you may, cast yourself down.
There is only One who can.
This is the word of the Lord.

DRYBONES (EZEKIEL 37:1-14)

My name is Ezekiel — but don't spread it around.
I'm not a particularly popular person.
You see, I've been blessed, or rather afflicted
with a constant, nagging and persistent obsession.
to tell the truth. So it shouldn't be surprising
    that I don't have many friends.

I belong to a particular nation. Call it Israel, if you must.
You and I, we are fellow citizens.
So many here believe in quick fixes to solve our problems—
    a pill, a new diet, "a different approach to religion", identity politics.
But I tell you,
the ills of our community go much deeper than that.
Let me tell you a little story to illustrate.

I had a really bizarre experience once—a vision, you might say.
I dreamed that

Adonai seized me
and I was brought by the spirit of Adonai
and put in the middle of a valley. It was full of bones.
There were very many, and very dry.

I wanted to scream, but he asked me to walk around, and look.
It seemed then that I was lifted out of that particular time and place
and was able to see with a bird's eye view all periods of history at once,
in a sweeping panorama.

Adonai led me into one corner of the valley, and it seemed to me
that I was at Auschwitz, and at Treblinka, and at Bergen-Belsen, and at
    Birkenau.
These bones were very dry, and they were piled up in heaps.
Someone, I knew, had been trying to bury them and hide them.
to deny their memory and their reality,

but the piles were too mountainous, they could not be hidden.
They blocked out the sunlight, and an acrid smoke filled my nostrils.
Here were the bones of two-thirds of the Jews of Europe.

And Adonai said to me,
You who also are mortal,
Can these bones be brought to life?

Then Adonai led me into a different corner of the valley
And it seemed to me that I was at Rwanda, and at Kosovo
and the bombed-out wasteland of Afghanistan

And there were very many bones, and they were very dry.

And Adonai said to me,
You who also are mortal,
Can these bones be brought to life?

Adonai led me into yet another corner of the valley,
and it seemed to me that I saw all the bones
of all the forgotten and abused of the cities and towns of America
frozen in subways, dead of addiction, women beaten and left to die,
others killed by a plague, their children
    killed by a plague
Black men killed with no justice in sight
And the bones of native peoples, not allowed to rest in their sacred ground.
And there were very many bones, and they were very dry.

And Adonai said to me,
You who also are mortal,
can these bones be brought to life?

I've told you of my inner impulse to tell the truth.
I looked around at all those bones. The world was a graveyard.
We had not learned from history, for this moment was our history.
Many of the bones had already disintegrated into dust, ashes to ashes.
Before me lay the death of hope.
Too late, my own voice sounded in my ears, Too late.

So when Adonai asked me the question, "Can these bones live?"
all the realism within me wanted to cry out, NO!
But I held my tongue.
I held my tongue, and the seconds ticked by,
and the wind whistled, rattling the dry bones.
And so when Adonai asked me, Can these bones live?

I answered, *Adonai, you are the one who knows.*

And then Adonai gave me the strangest command:
 to speak to the bones, to speak a word of hope.
I had to do it twice. I said, Arise.

The first time I spoke, the bones assembled into what looked like
    human beings,
But they were not alive. I almost said to Adonai,
"You see, it can never happen. The semblance of life is not life itself.
This is your job, isn't it? I don't believe in man-made miracles.
How can you expect me, of all people, to be optimistic?
We who turned our back on You have turned this world into a rank and stinking mess.
What do you expect me to say now? It didn't work the first time."

Then said Adonai,
"Although I know and speak all languages. I don't deal in colloquialisms.
I have given my breath to you as if you were the last one standing.
It is your responsibility to speak so these may understand,
Your responsibility to hope and to speak even in the place of death."

And then said Adonai,
Prophesy to the breath. Prophesy, mortal, and say to the breath:
Thus says Adonai: Come from the four winds, O breath,
And breathe upon these slain, that they may live.

I prophesied as Adonai commanded me, and the breath came into them,
And they lived, and stood on their feet, a vast multitude.

Then said Adonai,
You who also are mortal,
These bones are the whole house of my people. They say, our bones
    are dried up,
We are cut off completely. Therefore say to them,
Thus says Adonai: I am going to open your graves
And raise you from your graves, O my people.
And I will bring you back to your land.
And you shall know that I am Adonai,
When I open your graves, and raise you from your graves, O my people.
I will put my spirit within you, and you shall live.
And I will bring you home. Then you will know
That I, Adonai, have spoken, and I Adonai, have done it.
I can only work through you. Do you understand now?"

And then I understood. That was my task, to speak a word of hope,
despite my own hopelessness. Even here,
    at the end of all things.
Especially, here.

The dream began to fade.
I turned over on my cot and dreamed another . . . .
On the top of a hill, a vertical wooden rack
used in a certain era to torture and kill criminals.
Only a guard was there, and he told me
it was some Jewish Palestinian rabble-rouser
an excommunicate, thrown out of the synagogue.
who went around with a crowd of friends of dubious character.

He said, "Those Jews!", and spat on the ground.

I started to leave, but turned around
and saw the dawn was breaking, and what a glorious dawn it was,
the kind I've always loved.

A bird wheeled across the resplendent sky
I think it was a dove.

THE TIPSY PARSON

These also stagger from wine and reel from beer
Priests and prophets stagger from beer and are confused with wine
They reel from beer and stagger from hallucinations
They stumble when making decisions
And their tables are covered with vomit and filth is everywhere.

(. . .) Therefore the word of the Lord will become to them
as "do this" and "do that"
"Obey this rule" and "obey that rule"
"A little here" and "a little there"
And as a result, they will go and fall backward
And be injured and ensnared and taken.
(Isaiah 28:7–13)

This passage struck me when I was studying the Old Testament in my first year of seminary, which was also the last year of my drinking. The strange words burned into my mind like a firebrand. My college best friend had been murdered before I had left for New York, and once I was there, I had to walk four long city blocks to the West End Café. I would later walk home in a blackout. The men I hung around with were mostly older drunks who I knew wouldn't hurt me. I thought her death was my fault. That last year of my drinking, I was invited to a wedding in New Brunswick, and I hooked up with the bass player of the wedding band. I ended up in some bar at closing time, insisted on a drink and was escorted out physically by several men, and ended up with no shoes, in my wrap-around dress, my feet cut and bleeding, wandering around until I found the damn hotel. It was dawn. I looked at myself in the mirror and saw the ruin of a human being, but seeing, at the same time, the person I saw in a mirror as a child, the unique createdness of me. And soon I came to know what Luther meant when he said, "A person must be broken inside to receive the grace of God." (Thesis 18)

THE INTER-TESTAMENTAL PERIOD

Throughout the Law and the Prophets
God spoke and the people would not hear.
Nothing got their attention: floods, plagues, exile
A stiff-necked people.
It was abundantly clear.

Therefore, God paused and held her breath
then shrugged
and said to the angels,
Why not give it all?

Forget all your wanderings
throughout all the ages of the world before.
You who did not know me I forgive
I have decided to pay your debt
I give you my all now

I could not get through to you,
So now I will enter into you
And give you my image,
once and for all.
There is nothing else to be done.
Since I could not prevent your evil,
I will bear it
once and for all.

MELANIE

I met Melanie at the vape store a couple of years ago. She's got a big giving heart, a loud NY voice and doesn't give a damn, basically, about what people think of her. In her dark apartment, knick-knacks are carefully arranged on the mantel, framed pics of the grandkids who are going to be godknowswhere in a month, because her daughter Lisa is an addict and keeps getting shuttled back and forth between jail and rehabs and group homes. Melanie told me at one point that her daughter was pregnant and lost the baby but she wasn't sure why or how. Mel has a bf in jail, a total loser from her description of him, and she cries over him while reading Pinterest love sayings like "We've had a rough time, but you and me are meant to be and love will keep us together no matter what." She's got plaques on her walls like "Live. Laugh, Love". Meanwhile Lisa screams obscenities at her mom on speakerphone and I can clearly hear it while I'm sitting there trying to chill. And Melanie cries, and I've hit the vape a little too heavy, again.

About a year after this entry, Lisa died of an overdose. It's been a few months since her death. When people see Melanie out and about, getting cigarettes and groceries, she's constantly high on something. Everybody knows about her daughter, but she still asks people, Did you hear that Lisa died? All we can say is, I know. I'm really sorry to hear it.

HOW MANY LIKES?

Give us this day our daily bread, Starbucks and an iPhone
from which we glean a rush of recognition in a solipsistic world
playing in a sandbox with the other passive-aggressive toddlers
Late-night suicidal staring
at my 3 likes and her 28
while I painstakingly, post by post
sculpt a new face and a fake life
Desperately seeking salvation,
eyes glued
waiting for a drop of grace
from an upturned thumb
or the shape of a heart.

THIS LITTLE THING

"And now what we have left are faith, hope and love, but the greatest is love."

(1 Corinthians 13:13)

This little crying thing called Love
is greater than faith and hope.

We call faith that thing that makes us well,
The promise made to our forebears.

We call hope that thing that sustains us just until tomorrow
when we can begin to hope all over again, for just one day.

The tiny crying thing over there in the corner
is Love,
the little thing so despised
which never learns and always gives
and always
cries

NATURAL BORN WORLD SHAKER, "COOL HAND LUKE"

"Cool Hand Luke" (starring Paul Newman, directed by Stuart Rosenberg, 1967) is, like every work of art, culturally rooted, filmed during the Vietnam war era. Luke is a rebel with a telling history: he was back from some unspecified war, having earned the rank of Sergeant as a reward for distinguishing himself for bravery on the field. (We will see him sacrifice himself again.) The viewer isn't told the specifics of his discharge; all we know is that he returned home reduced to the status of "buck private". It's clear that he didn't care much for his former rank. Now, society has no place for him. We meet him drunk one night, caught by police for cutting the heads off of parking meters, in some unnamed American town — an act as purposeless as his past service during the war had seemed to him.

We next find Luke in a road prison, along with criminals much more hardened than himself, where he finds he is determined to shake up the status quo with its "rules and regulations". This is not simply anarchy for its own sake. In pushing the boundaries and testing all the limits of the system, Luke ultimately builds community in the most unlikely place, where the very least infraction of the "rules and regulations" leads to a night upright in "the box." Into this group of inmates who have built their own inner hierarchy where Dragline is the kingpin, Lucas bursts upon the scene, and says what he damn well pleases about what is just and what is being done terribly wrong, within both the power structures of the prison and that of the inmates.

Luke's entry galvanizes the community. He has something, an irresistible charisma. We see in his smile an invitation to do something that's never been done before: eating fifty eggs "in a hour", with Dragline and the rest excitedly putting up a dollar here, some cigarettes there, with a sharp division revealed between the believers and the unbelievers. Lucas, like a war hero, transforms the odious and backbreaking task of tarring a road into a contest of sheer delight: they complete the work two hours before quitting time, in what may seem to be a negligible victory over "The Man". But a victory nonetheless.

But there is much more here, and that "more" is squarely in line with the Judaic prophetic tradition, completed in the New Testament by the advent of the Christian Messiah. After swallowing the eggs, we see Luke lying on a table with a smile on his face, stretched out in the form of a cross. We may speculate that that smile emanates from his joy at bringing joy and purpose to the community, if only for a day in that miserable hopeless place. It was "something to do," he says. But it wasn't just "anything." He dared even to defy the laws of nature which called his belly to vomit forth, which would defeat his goal of winning the hearts of the men who had bet on him, as though for their lives, for just one day.

We can't forget his handle, which originated in his own words, "Sometimes nothing can be a real cool hand." *("And he {Christ} became nothing, so that we might become everything"* (Philippians 2:7). Janis Joplin, around the same time as the making of this film, famously sang "Freedom's just another word for nothing left to lose." As an itinerant first-century freak, Jesus had nowhere to lay his head. He had to have nothing in order to be free, and he had to be free in order to show others enmeshed in coercive power struggles and systems of authority that freedom was indeed possible. There was nothing for it, but for Luke to be defiant at the end, and joyful in the face of what was inevitably coming to him. The rest, like Dragline, had no such heart in them.

But they could always remember him, as we remember Christ, as a "natural born world shaker", a bringer of joy in impossible places, and acceptance, even joy, in the face of final annihilation.

TOMBS OF TWO GENERALS

Lee lies in polished silence of Vermont marble
With her voice, the guard caresses the weave of his camp blanket
At four corners, rebel flags still stand in grave salute
their tiny replicas bedeck the cold crypt
tossed through the bars by visitors in remembrance of a treasure lost,
    a living dream.

Defeat cherishes its heroes.

Whereas way up North
in a city unconnected to anything but itself
The victor Grant lies solitary
One guard, sleepy at his post
Careless of graffiti sullying the stones,
    litter on the cracked and shallow steps

while memory and meaning scatter
like so many autumn leaves.

WAR MACHINE

We are soldiers of the Unites States of America.
We have heard of Vietnam, we heard there was
    something called a "draft".
Many of us are too young, the 1960s are hypothetical.
Whether we signed up because there were nothing but dead ends at home
    in whatever American town
or because we believed in a mission that we didn't quite understand —
it doesn't matter, we are here now.

Here, we do not ask why.
What we have seen, we cannot unsee
just as you cannot see what tries us together
We lie for each other, we die for each other
We cover each others' backs.

That is not what we find when we get home.
That is not how we are rewarded for our service
by our loved ones who could not wait
could not hang in there long enough
the way we hang in for each other.
We do not ask why. We know the reason.
We enter into no "just war" debate.
That is for you to do,
who wake up fairly certain that there is breath to waste,
that you will live through this day.
That is what we are fighting for.

Sometimes, when we come home, we find no place to go.
Sometimes we return, back where the horror seems to have a purpose.
Not like home.

We fight for you,
who thank us, and revile us, and thank us again.
although you may not know why.

We do not ask why.

We are soldiers
of the United States of America.

CASUALTY

When I was around 17 in boarding school, I was heavy into drinking and drugs and wouldn't open a book except for the occasional glance at the poetry of Wallace Stevens. I made a friend named Stacey, gorgeous girl, loved her Tuinols. We started to hang with a bunch of bikers without bikes who are literally the worst kind of bikers. The guy I ended up with, Mike, got drafted and went to Vietnam. I always thought he was kind of a dumb guy. The only reason I was messing with that crowd was because they had weed and acid.

Mike wrote me a letter from Nam. He begged for a letter back. I blew it off, and a couple of months later learned he had been killed. I felt slightly guilty. Nothing that another 12 pack wouldn't fix.

That's what I thought at the time, anyway.

AMERICAN GUNS

Elderly couple gunned down at Shabbat.
Bury the dead, praise the heroes.

College kids partying to country music at a California downtown bar.
Bury the dead, praise the heroes.

46 in a Las Vegas massacre, heading for the club.
Bury the dead, praise the heroes.

High school kids in Florida
whose moms and dads will never be the same
Bury the dead, praise the heroes.

So the darkness spreads, the calculation has been made.
Their lives justify the feeling
of cold steel in the burning palm of a man who knows no meaning

only that of a lust for transcendent power exploding in his hand
and then, no more.

Bury your dead. Praise your heroes.

THE IMPECCABLE LOGIC OF JAMES HOLMES (THE "DARK KNIGHT" KILLER)

12 lives = 12 points
accrued by the Winner who has in himself
Only a value of 1.
By this logic, only the dead count
The wounded and bereaved are merely collateral damage.
By this logic, the only alternative to homicide is suicide.

The Devil is in the syllogism.
No one asks the question:
What is the value of 1?
Is it something other than a number?
Is it more than identity politics, or the millions of adjectives
that could be used to describe You?

Or is the 1 of infinite value
which no equation can convey or quantify?

Without the story
of the infinite hopes and fears, joys and disappointments of the 1,
it becomes a nullity
in the Dark Knight's dreamless sleep, not One
but Zero, the unholy Alpha
with the Absolute Value
of
Nothing.

LOST TIME

October flew past me.
I could only wanly smile at the straggling trick-or-treaters under my
   window.
in this late year.

All Saints Day dawned wet and dark this morning.
We have Thanksgiving, so that we will not feel so much
the chilling of our bones and the usual regrets
     in this late year
for love now long gone.
Then the vicious mindlessness of Christmas music
so we buy more to fill the emptiness.

My spirit sags this year, and yet I can still see
The tiny stubborn purple flowers pushing up from grass,
whose bold emerald defies the freezing rain that bends it to the ground
and will not submit to death, like my broken
     love for you.

Birds linger late on the Twischsawken River
gathering strength for the flight home.

Life resists its obliteration
at every moment
burning on like a candle in a deserted sanctuary

At least one soul, remembered
     in this late year.

A CONVERSATION: THE WOMAN AT THE WELL

(John 4:4–26)

It was necessary that Jesus go through Samaria. He came to a Samaritan village called Sychar. (Sychar is near the place that Joseph gave his son Jacob. It was Jacob's well.) Worn out and thirsty, Jesus sat down near the well. It was high noon. Then a Samaritan woman came to draw water. Jesus said to her, Give me something to drink.

(. . .) So then the Samaritan woman said to Jesus. You're a Jew, but you ask a woman from Samaria for a drink? Jews and Samaritans don't mix!

Jesus replied, If you could recognize God's gift when you see it, and the identity of the person who is asking you for a drink, you would be asking him, and he would have given you fresh {zoon} water The woman said, Look, Mister {kyrie}, you don't even have a bucket, and that well is deep. How are you going to access fresh water? You're not any more important than our ancestor Jacob who left this well to us to drink from . . . along with his children and his flocks—are you?

Jesus answered, Anyone who drinks from this water will be thirsty again. But whoever drinks from the water I give will never thirst again. But that water will become, inside them, like a fresh spring welling up unceasingly, to the end of time.

And the woman said to him, Master [kyrie], so that I'll never be thirsty, or have to come here to draw water again.

Jesus said to her, Go call your husband and come back, She said, I have no husband.

Jesus replied, That's true! You have seven 'husbands', and you're not even married to the one you have now.

(. . .) And the woman went into town and told everybody,

Come see the man who told me everything I ever did.

(Woman:)
Here I am at this stupid well again.
It's the same old routine every day.
Run out of water, go to the well, fill up my jug, go back.
Day after day, week after week, month after month, it's the same old thing.
It seems so pointless. I ask myself, why bother.
Except I'd die of thirst otherwise. No choice in the matter.
The sun is even hotter today.
It reminds me of my life. I never seem to get anywhere.
Take relationships, for example. I've had my share of those.
And I keep thinking, this one will be different.
I've finally found the man of my dreams.
And then what happens? He turns out to be a no-good worthless bum just like the rest of them.
I throw them all out, and I'm relieved for a while
and then that emptiness comes back.
And I never find what I think I'm looking for.

The truth is, I'm not getting any younger.
There's another one, now, hanging around the house.
It was good in the beginning, but now he's starting to annoy me.
I can see the end in sight, it's just no good anymore.
Why do I keep doing this? There must be something wrong with me.

Hmmm. I didn't see that man sitting over there.
I wonder if he heard me, talking to myself like a crazy woman.
I should go, but I don't have the energy.
Besides, he's sort of good-looking, in a scruffy kind of way.
Probably Jewish, though. That's why he's not talking to me.
Jews and Samaritans don't mix, like oil and water

Uh oh, here he comes.
I'm feeling butterflies in my stomach. Not sure why.

(Jesus:)
Give me a drink.

(Woman:)
Typical male.
Ordering women around without so much as a 'please.'
Besides, he's socially inept, and so inappropriate.
He shouldn't be talking to me, nor I to him.

(To Jesus:) How is it that you, a Jew, ask me, a woman of Samaria, for a drink?

(Jesus:)
If you knew the gift of God,
And who it is that is saying to you, Give me a drink,
You would have asked me,
And I would have given you living water.

(Woman, addressing the audience:)
Well, that just proves what I've been saying all along. Jews are strange people.
His words made no sense to me (. . .) and yet
I got a peculiar sensation when he was speaking to me.
And it wasn't that I was attracted to him, although as I said,
He's not bad looking.
It was just that his words reached into me, all the way
Into my heart. But my mind still wonders what he means.
(To Jesus:) Sir, you have no bucket, and the well is deep.
What do you mean by "living water"?
Most of the water around here is dead and brackish anyway.
You have to draw deeper, to get at the living streams.
Are you greater than Jacob, who gave us this well
and with his sons and his flocks drank from it?

(Jesus:)
Everyone who drinks from this water will be thirsty again.
(And I know all about your seven "husbands.")
But those who drink of the water that I will give them
will never be thirsty again.
The water that I will give them will become in them
a spring of water, gushing up to eternal life.

(Woman:)
Now I see.
Now I know, meeting you, why I've never been satisfied
Looking for love
in all the wrong places.
You are the Living Spring.
This is no accident.
Sir, give me this water, that my heart may never thirst again
that I might find myself again, or maybe for the first time.
Sir—or should I call you Lord,
Give me this water.

(All:)
Water of baptism. that brings the inner spring
Welling forth in the depths of all the adopted
For all their lives, forever, never-ending

Water that washes away the grime accrued in the soul
born and reborn

Water of life for those who die of thirst
replete with the brackish toxic sludge of the insatiable appetite of the unenlightened self

Water of joy, and I am a child again
kicking surf on the ocean sands of eternity
always ready to set sail once more, fishers of men
until we reach the other side.

12 STEP MEETING

I met JD in a 12 Step group meeting in New York City. I had been sober for about 2 years. Along with his heroin habit, JD was a cutter. He showed me the crude tattoos he had carved on his arm, when he was a junkie—probably to prove that he couldn't even feel it. JD was adopted at three years old. His biological father had been a child molester and blew his brains out at age 50.

Someone had shot JD in Central Park in the back, missing his spinal cord by a quarter of an inch. He had to have parts of both lungs removed. He had ended up a junkie hustler living in some kind of chicken coop type place on the Bowery, letting anyone do anything to him for a 5 dollar bag.

I shook his hand, and saw the light in his eyes, and I didn't even have to ask God how or why he had made it out alive.

SURVIVOR—
AN IMAGINARY THERAPIST'S NOTES

People in the group often say "you're as sick as your secrets."

The things you never tell anyone are the things that destroy you (although they may destroy you even if you tell). That's why Patient X told me about her family vacation home near Lake Erie. After the family would get back from the beach, the kids were allowed to take their wet bathing suits off behind the large house and run around naked until they were dry. It was fine up to a point . . . except that this practice was allowed to continue for too long with the boys now in their teens and she herself was around 10 years old.

One late afternoon, somehow they ended up in the woodshed next to the house. She didn't realize until she was an adult that the older brother must have lured her in there on purpose. She remembers ending up against a wooden wall naked, when her brother stuck his erect penis inside, with the other brother watching. She didn't think to say "stop" or try to get away, because she had always been afraid of him and his incessant bullying. After a short interval of this, he said, "Promise you won't tell anyone, and that you'll let us do this again when you're sixteen." She doesn't remember answering, or going inside the house for dinner, or what she covered herself with when she went into the house. Of course, she never told anyone.

The next summer, one of her brother's school friends visited. He started to touch her through her nightgown when they were watching TV and no one else was in the room.at the time. Silently, she stood up and walked out of the room. Patient told her sister about this when they were both adults. She was appropriately outraged.

That didn't help much. In her middle-aged years now, after a failed marriage, Patient's fantasies about these experiences dominate her mind, especially during masturbation. She can only think of the powerlessness that she felt, the debasement, now accompanied by a shudder of unspeakable desire. She tells me she can't open up to men and wears a suit of impenetrable emotional armor. She tells me that she "can't separate pain from pleasure and fear from desire." She is afraid that she will die this way, never having healed. She had loved her husband and had reached a certain level of intimacy with him, a level that now surprises her. After her marriage ended, she went through a series of relationships with broken and narcissistic men.

She wants to love again someday. But, she says, more pain will kill her. So she survives, alone. "But it's okay," she says. "I'm alright, I really am."

CHANCE MEETING OF POETS ON THE STREET*

Life is hard and I stay on my guard
But I never woke up in no graveyard
I woke up in prison with the Son of Sam
In Sing Sing he said he's met the great I Am
I woke up in a second floor psych ward
But I never woke up in no graveyard
I woke up when I gambled with no lucky cards
But I never woke up in no graveyard
I woke up when I cut myself with my own sword
But I never woke up in no graveyard
I woke up in a blackout slapped by the hand of God
But I never woke up in no graveyard
But I never woke up in no graveyard
I never woke up in no graveyard.

* This poem was co-written by Elishah Samoa and Alexandra Coe while we were talking on the street. A few months later in 2020, Elishah died of a heroin overdose. RIP Samoa

SOBER

The light you shined on me
in the dark days of blackouts and veins bruised from shooting up
was instantly blinding
the light that shocks the baby at its birth
the cold hard slap of reality that hurts
wailing being the first sign of life.

How do we survive this trauma of birth
except perhaps by an innate push
an urge, burning in our tiny pulsing hearts, to go forward, somehow
to find what is waiting for us in this frighteningly dazzling world?
Some of us
would prefer to live in the comfortable dark
until its shroud is cut away by a
    most rude God.
And the scar tissue of our broken hearts
become the stripes he received at the hands
    of those he came to save.

THREE UNDISCOVERED TUDOR MANUSCRIPTS

Marc Smeaton, 1512–1536, was a musician in the court of Henry VIII and a favorite of Queen Anne Boleyn. He was one of those accused of adultery with her, most likely falsely, and was put to death with the others. Smeaton was targeted first; court musicians were looked down upon, so that it was almost as shocking for the Queen to have an affair with a musician as it was for to have an affair with her brother George, who was also falsely accused and put to death. Queen Anne was executed in 1536. Her grave is at the shrine of St. Peter ad Vincula, London.

Mark Smeaton's Last Words

First I do assert without shame and in all God's truth that I loved Queen Anne. I loved her, knowing her to be one who best loved above all else her husband, lord and King, King Henry; who treated all who served in her retinue right well and generously. After her Lord and Master, My Lady loved music, especially the songs that her beloved had written for her, besotted in the first flush of their passion. When his favour for her abated for love of the Seymour girl, and when her fear and nervous exhaustion overcame her, late at night, she would bid me play for her, and she would sing passing clear and true to the note—always his songs. Then she would weep and bid me not leave her chamber until sleep had overtaken her. That is why these hideous rumours have come about, that I knew her as a husband knows his wife.

I have read the papers which condemn me. They are lies. They speak of one 'Marc', a despised court musician, whose bare given name stands stark among the list of those other condemned wretches with their full titles of nobility. Remember me, Marc, and the Lady who sang with him, and nothing more. We will be joined once again, in a place full of music, in a sphere of light, where fear and falsehood can never encroach.

Signed by my own hand. Marc Smeaton, court musician to Henry VIII.
The Tower of London
May 1536

Elizabeth I Before Henry VIII's Portrait

In everything you did, my kingly father, you bastardized and disowned me, kept me from lands, estates and well-kept bowers. You made me bow to my simpering sister Mary, the bloody bitch who threw me in the tower, and I survived on my own wit. You cut off her head, the one I cannot name. Yea, there were two who bore a fragile womb's blame, and forever made me fear the rule and spear of men, even while I could not resist them: the charming ones, volatile, like you yourself. I stand now before your painting; your baleful eyes mock me as they used. You made me suffer and I loved you well. I hate you well yet, and love you. I know in my anointed heart that God and the holy angels laughed and babbled Alleluia at my coronation, and that the people wept when I died the death of a monarch who surpassed you in love and in years, and reigned longer, even a weak a puling woman, among those you despised, stronger than my brother Edward, the star of your hope. I am the Virgin Queen.

A Possible Love Story: Sir Christopher Hatton on his Deathbed

Sir Christopher Hatton, 1540–1591, was a court favorite of Queen Elizabeth 1 and was named by her Lord Chancellor of England. She called him her Dancing Chancellor, because of his dancing skill. She often wore his gift to her, an ornament of jeweled bagpipes, on her sleeve.

Holdenby House, Northamptonshire
11 November, 1591

The doctors say the time will not be long, I am mortal ill, they know not what of. I think it be a sickness of the heart. I must put it down that the Queen visited me today, a favour I had longed for but not sought. My waning spirits rallied as I beheld her, older now, but still majestic, not dying, as I am. Her Grace spoke again of me as her Dancing Chancellour, and I chid her gently, reminding her I could no longer dance, and asked could she still love me. We laughed, and she took my hand and assured me it was so, and a tide of memories rushed in of times I used to partner her, as she danced so regal and beautiful in my eyes, not one misstep. I am fond to think that I brought Her Majesty half as much joy as she brought me in these short years of mine, not only in her service on the Privy Council but also in the dance, with the lords and ladies in their silks and satins and brocade, and a thousand gleaming tapers, and the music, such music. Before Her Grace departed I begged one final favour, that I be removed to Ely House to die, since I had pledged to her that I would not rest in this house one night until she too had rested here. She said she regretted it, and I told her I bore her no ill will, and she blessed and kissed me.

I cannot tell what it was between us, because I do not know how to tell it. But it was beautiful, as rare and as radiant as she.

Hatton
Lord Chancellour of England

WE, THE WOMEN

When the Sabbath was over, Mary Magdalene and Mary the mother of James and Salome brought spices, so that they might go and anoint [the body of Jesus]. And very early on the first day on the week, when the sun had risen, they went to the tomb. They had been saying to one another, "Who will roll away for us the stone at the entrance to the tomb?" When they looked, they saw that the stone, which was very large, had already been rolled away. When they entered the tomb, they saw a man . . . who said to them, "Do not be afraid. You are looking for Jesus of Nazareth, who was crucified. He is not here, he has risen. Go and tell his disciples that he has gone ahead of you to Galilee." So they went out and fled the tomb, for terror and amazement had seized them, and they said nothing to anyone, because they were afraid.

(Mark 16:1–9)

Who is going to roll away the stone for us at the entrance of the tomb?
We're all cried out, even though it is our duty to mourn. Mourning is always the province of women. But this death hits particularly hard.
We just wanted to say one final hello, to say I love you, and then goodbye to the only One who did not forget and despise us,
the women
the whores
the dancers and the singers
the cooks and the mothers
the teachers and the leaders that will be
those who must sit and listen.
It's the least we can do, and, empty and spent,
go home and try to get some sleep
And yet I am uneasy, because the day seems crowned with some new thing.
It frightens me.
I suppose we just wanted to make sure he was dead.
(I still can't quite believe it.

When someone dies you can never quite believe it. That's all this is, of
   course.)

Before we met him, we didn't think our lives were worth much
It was almost too hard to make it through each day
like trying to roll this stone uphill, every day
pushing them uphill forever
trying to try, trying to forgive, trying to forget, although
we never will forget him.
Those men he chose . . . you can't expect them to care about us now.
They will again reject us as unclean. We know this, we are not naïve.
We've never expected much from men anyway.

This man was different.

The stone has been moved! Someone must have stolen that racked and
   ruined body.
And who is this Stranger who says he has "gone ahead"?
I can't place his accent (. . .) He is not from here.
It must be a conspiracy. The authorities
are looking for us, too, no doubt.
They must have seen us with him, downtown somewhere.
The spices we bought —all wasted money.
Our religious duty is stripped from us
Just another slap in the face from men
in the wake of the incomprehensible news that he has "gone ahead"
Whatever that means.

How will we know him if we cannot see him?
How will we take his hand?
Surely you must understand (. . .) we are afraid.
And yet even now
I feel a gust of fresh air from the east
scattering the clouds
a whiff of something left in his wake . . .
It feels like hope, and suddenly,
I am not afraid.

(You know, sisters (. . .)
The way that Stranger spoke, his odd accent (. . .) Come to think of it,
It sounded just like Him.)

CHILD OF GOD?

Do I really believe it, when I say that I am a child of God?
(Ask yourself this, and
be silent for a moment before you answer.)

Am I really part of the family?
Or have I convinced myself that I am alien
a misplaced foundling, never formally adopted
forced on a family without their consent
through the secret back door of shame?

Do I see a Parent's face in mine
or only an ugliness that I despise
and have always despised
Never daring to claim the unmistakable family resemblance
its most resplendent features
and its beauty
in my own?

ONE STEP AHEAD—LIKE A ROLLING STONE

After the Sabbath, on the dawning of the first day of the week, Mary Magdalene and the other Mary went to see the tomb. You see, there had been a violent earthquake. A messenger of the Lord, sent from above, had rolled away the stone outside the tomb and was sitting on it. He looked like lightning, and his clothing was blindingly bright. The cemetery guards were seized with terror and froze like dead people.

But the messenger said to the women, There's no need to be terrified. Because I know you're looking for Jesus, the crucified. He is not here, he has risen, just as he predicted. See the place where he was? So go, quickly, and tell his disciples that he has risen from the dead, and has gone ahead of all of you to Galilee. That is where you will meet him again.

So the women ran from the tomb, terrified and ecstatic at the same time, running to tell the disciples, and all of a sudden they met Jesus.
He said,
Chairete.

(Matthew 28:1–10)

"At the dawning of the first day of the week."
Before the day begins.
Dawn is a time when the day lies ahead of us.
A blank slate, a sheet of gleaming white paper, tabula rasa
a sheet not yet written upon with words, with old, old words.
The day lies ahead like a world unexplored
replete with possibility. That is how Easter begins.

The women came—so it is said—to view the tomb.

How many gravestones, how many tombs
How many places of memorial are viewed every day throughout the world?
What do we come looking for at the tomb, at any tomb?
We come to remember
to cope with an end

to come to closure, as they say.

We come, too, to face ourselves
To shrug off the nagging guilt, to make sense of the past.

We come to try to understand the word 'goodbye'.

And so, perhaps armed with the tools for a brass rubbing,
We trace the outline of a memory, with flowers and with tears.
It is in the natural order of things.

We go on living, wanting so much less than Life.

But then an earthquake is reported, a fearsome disturbance
not normally associated with easter
dislodging the familiar comfortable imagery of butterflies sweetly
   emerging
from cocoons.
An earthquake makes us run and hide. It does not make us smile.
Objects in our lives that we have carefully arranged
become dislodged, upsetting our protective architecture, threatening to
   tear down
the entire structure.

(Incidentally,
Did you see that strange man in white, actually sitting on the tombstone?
So inappropriate. Is nothing
sacred?
Nothing out of the ordinary should happen here. Nothing unexpected.)

We go on living, wanting so much less than Life.

That Stranger said, "Do not be afraid." How did he know?
We are afraid that his body has been stolen.
We are afraid of the authorities.
We are afraid that we will be stripped of our women's duty to mourn
the duty of all women since time began.

Then the Stranger said, "He goes before you, to Galilee."
What if this is true? It does make sense, in a way.
That Nazarene . . . He was always one step ahead.
He was always forgiving when we thought he should be condemning
or burning with a holy wrath when we thought he'd go along with things
or doing something frivolous like turning water into wine
at some random wedding. It turned out to be a great party.
I'll never forget it.

First he'd be disputing in the synagogue, brilliantly! —
then drinking with the scum of Palestine.
You could never catch up with him. He surprised us constantly. But
This
is a bit too surprising.
Here we are, grieving,
somehow comfortable with the pain that he has shaken off
like a dead skin.

Well, he always liked to travel. He was never one
to let the grass of a tomb grow under his feet
Like a rolling stone.
Yes, it all makes sense. He is not here.

The Stranger told us to go quickly, and tell the rest.
After we gave the guards some good strong wine we took off.
It was when we were running that we met him again,
running to tell.
He greeted us with one word, "Chairete!"
In your language it is untranslatable.
It was "hello" and "joy" at the same time.
It was like the beginning of a love that never fades or lessens.
It was like the greeting of someone
you have longed all your life to meet.
It was like the return of someone
for whom you had stopped hoping
It was the beginning of all beginnings.
Chairete! That greeting
still sounds in my heart.

Yes, it was when we were running that we met him
Running to tell.

And so we do to this day
Run to spread his word of joy and greeting while we can
before the Night comes
for the time is short

We still, to this day, and so will you
do what the Stranger said.
This is our call, no longer tending
    the graves of our hearts.

For He was a man one step ahead,
A man of the open road
leading on Forever.
That's what we want to be. Yes.
That's what we want to be.

END